HAL•LEONARD
INSTRUMENTAL
PLAY-ALONG

AUDIO
ACCESS
INCLUDED

PLAYBACK+
Speed • Pitch • Balance • Loop

T0083311

Disney

ENCANTO

2   All of You

4   Colombia, Mi Encanto

6   Dos Oruguitas

5   The Family Madrigal

8   Surface Pressure

10   Waiting on a Miracle

12   We Don't Talk About Bruno

14   What Else Can I Do?

Audio arrangements by Peter Deneff

To access audio visit:
www.halleonard.com/mylibrary

Enter Code
4199-0233-7530-0086

Disney characters and artwork © Disney Enterprises, Inc.

ISBN 978-1-70516-355-9

HAL•LEONARD®

Visit Hal Leonard Online at
www.halleonard.com

Contact us:
Hal Leonard
7777 West Bluemound Road
Milwaukee, WI 53213
Email: info@halleonard.com

In Europe, contact:
Hal Leonard Europe Limited
42 Wigmore Street
Marylebone, London, W1U 2RN
Email: info@halleonardeurope.com

In Australia, contact:
Hal Leonard Australia Pty. Ltd.
4 Lentara Court
Cheltenham, Victoria, 3192 Australia
Email: info@halleonard.com.au

ALL OF YOU

Clarinet

Music and Lyrics by
LIN-MANUEL MIRANDA

COLOMBIA, MI ENCANTO

CLARINET

Music and Lyrics by
LIN-MANUEL MIRANDA

THE FAMILY MADRIGAL

CLARINET

Music and Lyrics by
LIN-MANUEL MIRANDA

DOS ORUGUITAS

CLARINET

Music and Lyrics by
LIN-MANUEL MIRANDA

SURFACE PRESSURE

CLARINET

Music and Lyrics by
LIN-MANUEL MIRANDA

WAITING ON A MIRACLE

CLARINET

Music and Lyrics by
LIN-MANUEL MIRANDA

WE DON'T TALK ABOUT BRUNO

CLARINET

Music and Lyrics by
LIN-MANUEL MIRANDA

Moderate Cha-Cha

WHAT ELSE CAN I DO?

CLARINET

Music and Lyrics by
LIN-MANUEL MIRANDA